Essential Ecuadorian Recipes

An Illustrated Cookbook of South American Dish Ideas!

Table of Contents

Introduction

What types of meats, vegetables, fruits and other native foods are found in genuine Ecuadorian meals?

Ecuador is known for bananas, sure, and there are lots of recipes that include bananas. But that's not all the country has to offer. They eat many starchy foods like yuca, rice, pasta, breads and potatoes. These may be included in rice platters or delicious bowls of soup served in any one of their meals.

Across Ecuador, those ingredients and others are staples of the native diet. Plantains are also featured often in dishes that originate in this South American country. They do much of their seasoning with Aji, a hot sauce made from spicy chili peppers. Stews and soups are traditional recipes, as are various types of ceviche recipes.

Ecuadorians enjoy many types of beverages made since the early days of the country. One of the favorites is aguardiente, a spirit made with pure sugar cane. Another popular drink is canelazo, and it has a base of aguardiente.

You may enjoy drinkable yogurt that is eaten often in the country. It comes in lots of fruit flavors and may be served with pan de yuca, which is a gooey, puffy bread made with cassava flour. Turn the page and learn more about Ecuador's tasty dishes...

1 – Ecuadorian Breakfast Fruit Salad

The name of this dish translates to "eat drink". The tropical salad is created using citrus juices, along with bananas and papaya. It's refreshing on those hot summer days.

Makes 8 Servings

Cooking + Prep Time: 20 minutes + 1/2 hour chilling time

Ingredients:

- 4 1/2 cups of orange juice, fresh
- 1 peeled, then seeded diced papaya, large
- 1 peeled, then cored diced pineapple
- 6 peeled, diced bananas

- As desired: honey or sugar
- To serve, optional: whipped cream with honey

Instructions:

1. Combine bananas, papaya and pineapple in large glass or Pyrex bowl.

2. Mix in orange juice and add honey or sugar, as desired.

3. Serve promptly or chill for 1/2 hour if it's a particularly hot day. That will make it most refreshing.

2 – Ecuadorian Huevos Rancheros

Huevos rancheros are served in many countries, and in Ecuador they are made with black beans in a tortilla bowl, accompanied by garlic and onions. They are topped with fried eggs, cheese, sour cream and avocado.

Makes 2 Servings

Cooking + Prep Time: 1/2 hour

Ingredients:

- 3 minced garlic cloves
- 1 chopped onion, medium
- 1 cup of rinsed, drained beans, black
- 2 tortilla bowls, pre-packaged
- 4 eggs, large
- 1/2 cup of shredded cheese, cheddar
- 1 peeled, then pitted thinly sliced avocado
- 2 tbsp. of sour cream

Instructions:

1. Heat skillet on med. heat. Add garlic and onion. Stir while cooking till they are translucent and softened. This takes about eight to 10 minutes.

2. Combine the beans with the cooked garlic and onion in bowl. Place the tortilla bowls inside serving bowls. Spoon the bean and onion mixture into the tortilla bowls.

3. Heat the skillet on med-low. Crack the eggs into the skillet. Cook to your desired level. Place the eggs on the bean mixture and sprinkle with the cheese.

4. Cook each tortilla bowl inside serving bowl in microwave till cheese melts. Top each with avocado slices and sour cream. Serve.

3 – Fried Cheese Breakfast Empanadas

These are the favorite type of empanadas made in Ecuador. They fill them with grated cheese and sometimes onions. Then they are fried and sprinkled with cane sugar.

Makes 8-10 Servings

Cooking + Prep Time: 45 minutes + 1 hour chilling time

Ingredients:

- 15 medium sized empanada discs, store-bought
- For cheese filling cooking:

- 2 1/2 cups of cheese, grated – you may use Monterey Jack, mozzarella or other cheese that is easily melted
- Optional: 1 cup of white onion, chopped finely
- To sprinkle: 1/2 cup of sugar
- To fry: oil

Instructions:

1. Mix chopped onions and grated cheese together.

2. Spoon cheese filling in middle of empanada discs.

3. Fold empanada discs. Fold edges and use fork to seal.

4. Chill empanadas for an hour or more, to seal them more fully and prevent any leaks.

5. Fry empanadas in fry pan. Use enough oil that it covers 1/2 of empanadas at a minimum. Allow the oil to get quite hot. Fry empanadas till they have turned golden brown on both sides.

6. Place empanadas on plate lined with paper towels and allow excess oil to drain. Generously sprinkle them with sugar. Serve while warm.

4 – Tigrillo Egg Plantain Breakfast

This Ecuadorian specialty breakfast dish is made with green plantains that are mashed and then scrambled with eggs and queso fresco. It's sometimes served for brunch or lunch, too.

Makes 1 Serving

Cooking + Prep Time: 30 minutes

Ingredients:

- 1 green plantain, whole
- 2 tbsp. of butter, salted
- 2 ounces of cheese, feta

- 2 pasteurized eggs, whole
- 1 pinch each kosher salt ground pepper
- To serve: 1/2 sliced avocado

Instructions:

1. Bring pot of filtered water to a boil. Peel plantain: cut ends off and slit skin lengthways. Peel skin off using your hands.

2. Next, cut plantain into four or five medium-sized pieces. Cook in boiling water for 18-20 minutes or so.

3. Remove plantain from water. Don't discard the water. Mash plantain with fork or potato masher.

4. Cut cheese in cubes (small). Whisk eggs in medium bowl.

5. Heat the butter in fry pan. Add mashed plantain. Add reserved water as needed so it will remain soft and not dry out. Once you have a mushy consistency, add cheese. Cook till it's soft, about two or three minutes.

6. Move cheese plantain mash to sides of pan. Leave space open in center of pan. Then pour whisked eggs in open space. Scramble for a minute with spatula. When eggs begin

scrambling but still have a creamy texture, combine with remainder of ingredients.

7. Stir mixture till eggs have cooked fully. Season as desired. Serve.

5 – Plantain Breakfast Dumplings

This dish starts with dumplings made from green plantains. They are then stuffed with chorizo or cheese and fried till they're crispy.

Makes 6-8 Servings

Cooking + Prep Time: 1 3/4 hour

Ingredients:

- 4 peeled, chunk-cut plantains, green
- 2 tbsp. of oil, sunflower

- 4 to 5 tbsp. of butter, unsalted
- 1 tbsp. of chili powder or hot pepper
- 1 tsp. of cumin, ground
- 1 cup of cheese, grated
- Salt, kosher, as desired
- Ground peanuts, optional

Instructions:

1. Melt butter on med. heat in large sized sauté pan.

2. Add chunks of plantain. Cook for 35-40 minutes, till they're quite soft, turning them every 10 minutes or so. They should become a bit golden in color, yet not overly crispy.

3. Sprinkle cooked plantains with cumin, chili powder and kosher salt.

4. Transfer pieces of plantain to bowl while they're hot, being careful.

5. Mash plantains till the consistency of the dough is chunky.

6. Form balls a bit smaller than tennis balls using dough.

7. Press a hole in centers of balls. Fill with cheese. Press filling gently into hole. Then cover filling. Recreate the ball shape.

8. Next, heat oil on high. Add plantain dumplings. Fry till crispy and golden.

9. Transfer plantains to paper towels and drain excess grease. Serve promptly.

Ecuadorians have many delectable choices for lunch, dinner, side dishes and appetizers. Here are some favorites...

6 – Ecuadorian Chicken Rice

This dish is known as arroz con pollo, meaning rice with chicken. It's a wonderful meal to serve your family. It varies from one household to the next, but they all seem to be delicious.

Makes 4-6 Servings

Cooking + Prep Time: 50 minutes

Ingredients:

For the chicken

- 3 tbsp. of oil, olive
- 1 fryer/boiler chicken, 2 1/2 to 3 lbs., cubed

- 1/2 cup flour to dredge in
- Salt, kosher, as desired
- Pepper, black, ground, as desired
- Paprika, sweet
- Rice
- 1 chopped medium onion, yellow
- 2 tbsp. of oil, olive
- 1 minced clove of garlic
- 2 cups of white rice, long or med-grain
- 3 cups of stock, chicken
- 1 heaping tsp. of tomato paste, low sodium
- 1 pinch oregano
- 1 tsp. of salt, kosher

Instructions:

1. Heat 3 tbsp. of oil in large size skillet with lid, on med-high.

2. Pour flour into wide bowl. Mix in kosher salt, ground pepper paprika, as desired. Dredge the pieces of chicken lightly in this mixture. Place in pan.

3. Cook for several minutes per side, till chicken browns. Remove pieces from the pan. Set them aside.

4. Add rice to pan. Add additional oil if you need it. Stir rice and coat it with oil. Allow rice to brown.

5. Add the garlic and onion. Cook them in rice mixture and stir frequently, till onions are softened.

6. Place the pieces of chicken with the skin side facing up, on top of rice.

7. In separate bowl, mix stock, tomato, oregano and salt together. Pour this over chicken and rice.

8. Bring to simmer and reduce the heat down to low. Cover the pan. Allow to cook for 20 to 25 minutes, till chicken and rice are done.

9. Fluff rice. Season as desired. Serve.

7 – Ecuadorian Potato Corn Salad

When you read the ingredients for this dish, you'll wonder if they can ALL work together well. They do! It's a great recipe for the summertime.

Makes 4 Servings

Cooking + Prep Time: 1/2 hour

Ingredients:

- 1/3 cup of oil, olive
- 3 tbsp. of lime juice, fresh
- 3 tbsp. of pineapple juice
- 1 tsp. of ancho chili powder, dried
- 1/4 tsp. of salt, kosher
- 1/4 tsp. of pepper, ground
- 1 1/4 pounds of potatoes, red or purple
- 1 cup of corn kernels, fresh
- 1 cup of snow peas
- 3 carrots, medium
- 1 celery stalk
- 1 cup of drained pineapple tidbits
- 2 heads of lettuce, Boston
- 2 eggs, hardboiled
- 2 tbsp. of chopped parsley, fresh

Instructions:

1. Slice snow peas in thirds. Grate carrots. Dice celery. Chop eggs.

2. Mix lime and pineapple juices with olive oil, kosher salt, ground pepper and chili powder in jar. Blend by shaking well and set the jar aside.

3. Scrub potatoes. Pierce them using a fork and arrange them in a loose circle in microwave oven. Cook on the high setting for four minutes. Turn them over. Microwave for four minutes on that side, too. Remove potatoes from microwave. Wrap in kitchen towel.

4. Place snow peas and corn in glass bowl. Cover. Microwave on the high setting for two to three minutes, till peas have turned a bright shade of green.

5. Add and stir pineapple, carrots and celery. Allow to cool down to lukewarm. Mix with 1/2 prepared dressing and place in refrigerator.

6. Arrange lettuce on four individual plates. Peel, then slice the potatoes. Arrange in circle at outside lettuce edges. Place corn mixture in middle of lettuce. Sprinkle using parsley and chopped eggs. Drizzle with remainder of dressing. Serve.

8 – Ecuadorian Pickled Onions

These onions are a superb condiment for many types of dishes. They are tossed with citrus juice and are delicious when sprinkled over a ceviche.

Makes 1 quart

Cooking + Prep Time: 35 minutes + 3+ hours chilling time

Ingredients:

- 2 thinly sliced onions, red
- 3-4 limes, fresh, juice only
- Kosher salt ground pepper, as desired

Instructions:

1. Pour onions in medium bowl. Cover with boiling water and allow to stand for 15-18 minutes. Drain. Rinse onions using cool water.

2. Mix onions with fresh lime juice, kosher salt ground pepper.

3. Refrigerate for three or more hours before you use them for a dish you're serving.

9 – Ecuadorian Vegetable Soup

I first tasted this dish a couple years back. It sounds so simple and it is, but it's incredibly tasty and filling. It serves up well after freezing, too.

Makes 4-6 Servings

Cooking + Prep Time: 1 1/4 hour

Ingredients:

- 1/2 cup of quinoa, raw
- 2 tbsp. of oil, olive
- 2 cups of onions, chopped
- 1 tsp. of salt, kosher
- 1 cup of potato, diced

- 1 cup of chopped bell peppers, red
- 1 tsp. of coriander, ground
- 1 tsp. of cumin, ground
- 1 tsp. of oregano, dried
- 1/2 tsp. of pepper, ground
- 1 cup of vegetable stock or water
- 1 1/2 cups of chopped tomatoes, fresh
- 1 cup of squash, yellow
- 1 tbsp. lemon juice, fresh

Instructions:

1. Rinse quinoa well in fine strainer under cold running water and set it aside so it can drain.

2. Heat oil in large pot.

3. Add onions and kosher salt to pot. Cover. Cook on med. for five minutes, stirring occasionally.

4. Add bell pepper, potatoes, drained quinoa, cumin, coriander, pepper, oregano, tomatoes and vegetable stock or water. Stir and combine well.

5. Cover pot. Bring to boil, then lower heat and allow to simmer for 10-12 minutes.

6. Add yellow squash. Cover. Allow to simmer for 18-22 minutes more, till veggies become tender.

7. Add lemon juice. Stir and combine well. Serve.

10 – Pork and Hominy Stew

This is a wonderful hominy recipe. Pork stew is an uncomplicated dish to serve, and you'll be getting protein and veggies in a single dish.

Makes 6 Servings

Cooking + Prep Time: 50 minutes

Ingredients:

- 2 tbsp. of chili powder, ancho
- 2 tsp. of oregano, dried
- 1 1/2 tsp. of paprika, smoked
- 1 tsp. of cumin, ground
- 1/2 tsp. of salt, kosher
- 1 1/2 lbs. of 1/2" cut pork tenderloin
- 1 tbsp. of oil, olive
- 2 cups of onion, chopped
- 1 1/2 cups of chopped bell pepper, green
- 1 tbsp. of garlic, minced
- 2 1/2 cups of chicken broth, low sodium, fat-free
- 1 x 28-oz. can of drained hominy
- 1 x 14 1/2 oz. can of undrained, diced tomatoes, fire roasted

Instructions:

1. Combine the first five ingredients in large sized bowl. Set 1 1/2 tsp. of the spice mixture to the side.

2. Add the pork to the rest of the spice mixture in medium bowl. Toss well and coat fully.

3. Heat 2 tsp. of oil in large pot on med-high. Add the pork mixture. Cook and stir occasionally for five minutes, till pork has browned. Remove the pork from pot and set it aside.

4. Add 1 tsp. oil to pot. Add garlic, onion and bell pepper. Sauté for five minutes and stir occasionally, till they are tender. Return the pork to the pot. Add 1 1/2 tsp. of spice mixture, tomatoes, broth and hominy and bring to boil. Cover pot partially and reduce the heat. Simmer for 25-30 minutes. Serve.

11 – Sweet Baked Plantains

This recipe is intended to be made with plantains that are very ripe. When they are picked, plantains are usually still green, but they need to have turned to yellow with some black skin to be perfect for this dish.

Makes 4 Servings

Cooking + Prep Time: 25 minutes

Ingredients:

- 4 plantains, ripe – with yellow skin and black spots
- Non-stick spray

Instructions:

1. Preheat the oven to 450F.

2. Coat baking sheet with non-stick spray.

3. Cut ends off plantains. Peel them.

4. Slice plantains on diagonal in 1/2" slices.

5. Arrange the slices in one layer. Coat with non-stick spray.

6. Bake and turn occasionally for 12-17 minutes, till plantains are tender and golden brown in color. Serve.

12 – South American Black Bean Stew

You can enjoy this wonderful and simple stew any time you like. You can even leave out the meat and it still tastes great.

Makes 6 Servings

Cooking + Prep Time: 3/4 hour

Ingredients:

- 1 tbsp. of oil, canola
- 1/4 lb. of chopped sausage, chorizo
- 1/3 lb. of chopped ham, cooked

- 1 chopped onion, medium
- 2 minced garlic cloves
- 1 x 1-lb. peeled, diced sweet potato
- 1 diced bell pepper, red, large
- 2 x 14 1/2 oz. cans of tomatoes in their juice, diced
- 1 diced small chili pepper, green, hot
- 1 1/2 cups of water, filtered
- 2 x 16-oz. cans of rinsed, drained beans, black
- 1 peeled, de-seeded, diced mango
- 1/4 cup of chopped cilantro, fresh
- 1/4 tsp. of salt, kosher

Instructions:

1. Heat oil in large sized pot on med. heat. Cook ham and chorizo for two to three minutes.

2. Place onion in pot. Cook till it is tender. Then add and stir garlic. Cook till tender. Add and mix water, chili pepper, tomatoes and juice, bell pepper and sweet potatoes. Bring to boil and reduce the heat down to low. Cover pot. Simmer for 15-18 minutes, till you have tender sweet potatoes.

3. Stir beans into pot. Leave pot uncovered and cook till beans heat through. Then mix in cilantro and mango. Season as desired and serve.

13 – South American Cilantro Rice

This is a perfect side to serve with a main chicken dish. You can add green onions to its cilantro if you like, and the rice tastes great when it is cooked with chicken stock.

Makes 6 Servings

Cooking + Prep Time: 40 minutes

Ingredients:

- 2 x 4-oz. halved chicken breasts, boneless, skinless
- 1 bunch of cilantro, fresh – remove stems
- 1/2 cup of water, filtered

- 1 tbsp. of oil, vegetable
- 1 tbsp. of garlic, minced
- 1/4 cup of chopped carrots, frozen
- Optional: 1/4 cup of peas, frozen
- 1 tbsp. of cumin, ground
- Kosher salt ground pepper, as desired
- 1 cup of white rice, uncooked

Instructions:

1. Place chicken in large sized sauce pan. Add filtered water sufficient to cover the chicken.

2. Bring to boil. Cook for 15-18 minutes, till chicken is fully done. Dice the chicken and reserve its cooking liquids.

3. Puree cilantro in 1/2 cup of water in food processor.

4. Heat oil in sauce pan. Cook the garlic till browned lightly. Add two cups cooking liquid. Stir in rice, peas, carrots, chicken pieces, cilantro puree and cumin. Season as desired.

5. Bring to simmer and cover pan. Cook over low till liquid is absorbed and rice becomes tender. This usually takes 15-20 minutes or so. Serve.

14 – Patacones

These fried plantain slices are made using green plantains. They are thicker than plantain chips and offer a wonderful taste.

Makes 16 Servings

Cooking + Prep Time: 1/2 hour

Ingredients:

- 4 plantains, green
- Oil, vegetable
- Salt, kosher

Instructions:

1. Peel the plantain. Cut width-ways in three or four pieces.

2. Heat 1 inch of oil over med. heat till hot.

3. Fry the pieces of plantain for three minutes per side, till they are a golden color. Remove them from the pan. Place on plate with paper towels.

4. Flatten plantains. Place in heated oil again. Fry till both sides of plantains are a golden brown in color.

5. Drain plantains on plate covered with paper towels. Sprinkle with kosher salt and serve promptly.

15 – Fried, Stuffed Cheese Cassava Balls

These muchines de yuca are cassava balls that have a crunchy texture on the outside and a savory, soft filling. It can be served as a side dish or an appetizer.

Makes 12 Servings

Cooking + Prep Time: 45 minutes

Ingredients:

For the filling

- 1 cup cheese, grated – Swiss, mozzarella or Monterey Jack work well
- For cassava balls
- 1 lb. of peeled, grated cassava (yuca)
- 1 grated onion
- 1 egg, large
- Kosher salt ground pepper, as desired
- To fry: oil

Instructions:

1. Melt the cheese filling and set it aside till needed.

2. Mix cassava, egg and onion in large sized bowl. Season as desired.

3. Place roughly 1/4 cup of cassava mixture in your hand. Form an indentation in middle of blob using your thumb.

4. Place 1 tbsp. cheese filling in the indentation. Fold cassava over and enclose the filling.

5. Form cassava into oval ball. Squeeze out excess moisture, if any. Set ball aside. Repeat with remainder of cassava and cheese filling.

6. Heat one to two inches oil in deep skillet on med-high till it is shimmering.

7. Fry cassava balls in batches of three or four till they are cooked through and golden brown in color, about four to six minutes. Turn so both sides will brown.

8. Remove cassava balls to plate lined with paper towels. Serve while still hot.

16 – Langostino Ceviche

Langostino have the appearance of crawfish or small lobster, and you can substitute either of those in this ceviche. After it's marinated in jalapeno, lime juice, red onion and garlic, it is great to pair with tortilla chips.

Makes 4 Servings

Cooking + Prep Time: 50 minutes + 2 hours marinating time

Ingredients:

- 1 pound of langostino meat, cooked
- 1/2 onion, red

- 8 juiced limes, fresh
- 1 tsp. of crushed oregano, Mexican
- 2 peppers, serrano
- 1/2 bunch of cilantro, chopped finely + 5 extra sprigs of cilantro
- 1 to 2 tbsp. of oil, olive
- 3 lightly crushed cloves of garlic
- Salt, kosher

Instructions:

1. Cut onion into halves. Remove outer skin. Trim top off. Cut down center to root. Slice the onion thinly. Place slices in bowl. Add salt. Cover with juice of one lime and warm water. Allow to rest for 10-12 minutes, then drain and rinse with cool water.

2. Place cooked langostino in bowl. Add clove of garlic, cilantro sprigs, hot peppers, onion slices, remainder of lime juice, kosher salt and dry oregano. Cover the bowl. Place in the refrigerator to marinate for two hours or so.

3. Remove hot pepper, clove of garlic and cilantro sprigs. Discard them.

4. Add oil and chopped cilantro to marinated onions and langostino. Mix thoroughly and incorporate well. Season as desired. Serve with fresh, salted tortilla chips.

17 – Peanut Potato Soup

This soup is economical, as well as being tasty and nourishing. It is usually made with chicken or beef ribs, but it can stand alone as a veggie soup, too.

Makes 4-6 Servings

Cooking + Prep Time: 2 1/2 hours

Ingredients:

- 4 garlic cloves
- 1 onion, large

- 2 medium carrots
- 2-3 tbsp. of oil, vegetable + extra to fry potato sticks
- 3/4 lb. of short ribs, beef
- 1/2 tsp. of cumin, ground
- 1 tsp. of oregano, ground
- 6 cups of stock, beef
- 1 cup of raw peanuts, unsalted
- 1 cup of water, filtered
- 4 yellow potatoes, medium
- 1/2 cup of rice
- Kosher salt ground pepper, as desired
- 1/2 cup of peas, frozen or fresh
- For garnishing: 1-2 tbsp. of parsley, chopped
- Optional: pepper sauce, hot

Instructions:

1. Mince onions and garlic finely. Peel carrots. Dice into small pieces and set onions and carrots aside.

2. Pour oil in large sized pot on med. heat. Add beef ribs. Briefly sauté them till all sides are browned.

3. Add carrots, garlic, onions, oregano and cumin. Continue stirring and cooking for three to four additional minutes. Add beef stock. Bring to simmer.

4. Place peanuts in your food processor. Add 1 cup of filtered water. Process the peanuts till they have formed a thick and mostly smooth paste. Use more water if you need it. Add this paste to soup. Stir thoroughly. Cover the pan and allow soup to simmer for about one hour.

5. Peel potatoes. Reserve one for match sticks.

6. Slice remaining three potatoes in small one to two inch wedges. Add to soup. Add more water or stock as needed. Cover. Simmer till potatoes are cooked well. Mash them gently in soup.

7. Remove the ribs from soup. Allow them to cool. Remove meat from the bones. Add meat back into soup. Add rice. Simmer for 20-25 more minutes.

8. Season soup as desired. Add peas, reduce heat down to low.

9. Cut the last potato in match sticks. Heat 1/2 inch oil in small sized pan. Cook potato sticks till browned. Remove and drain them on paper towels. Season as desired.

10. Ladle soup into bowls. Garnish with the chopped parsley and matchstick fries. Serve.

18 – Avocados with Shrimp

The avocadoes in this dish are stuffed with shrimp salad. It is a very simple recipe to make, and still comes off as refreshing and delicious.

Makes 8 Servings

Cooking + Prep Time: 35 minutes

Ingredients:

- 3 avocados, fresh
- 1 cup mayonnaise, reduced fat

- 1/4 cup ketchup, low sodium
- 2 spoons full of chopped olives
- 1 tbsp. of minced red pepper
- 1 tbsp. of minced onion, red
- 1 hard-boiled egg, large
- 2 spoons full of minced parsley
- 2 spoons full of chopped peppers, jalapeno
- 17 1/2 ounces of shrimp shoddy

Instructions:

1. Make sauce using all ingredients except avocado and shrimp. Season as desired and add in the shrimp.

2. Spread avocados and season them as desired, too.

3. Fill avocados with shrimp. Place on lettuce leaves. Serve.

19 – Shrimp Tomato Sauce Ceviche

This ceviche employs red onions and nutty kernels of corn to create a taste sensation that's hard to forget. You can serve it with toasted cancha, too.

Makes 4-6 Servings

Cooking + Prep Time: 45 minutes

Ingredients:

- 2-3 cups of sm-med shrimp, pre-cooked
- 1/2 onion, red

- 1 lime, fresh, juice only
- 1/4 cup of orange juice, fresh squeezed
- 1/2 cup of ketchup, low sodium
- 1 tbsp. of vinegar, white
- 1 tbsp. of sugar, granulated
- 1 cup of corn kernels, fresh
- 1/4 cup of cilantro leaves, packed

Instructions:

1. Slice onion as thinly as you can. Slice it with its cut side laying face down.

2. Place onion slices in bowl of cool, lightly salted water. Allow to soak for 20-25 minutes.

3. Cook corn in pot of salted water at boil till barely tender. Drain. Rinse using cold water.

4. De-vein cooked shrimp. Trim tails off. Place in bowl.

5. Drain the onions. Use cold water to rinse. Add the corn and onions to the bowl with shrimp.

6. Whisk orange juice, lime juice, vinegar, ketchup and sugar together. Toss this mixture with onions, shrimp and corn. Season as desired.

7. Chill the shrimp till you want to serve them. Toss them with cilantro. Serve.

20 – Ecuadorian Chicken Soup

This recipe has a long prep time, but it's easy to make. The final taste is very much worth the time spent, as it's truly a homemade dish.

Makes 8 Servings

Cooking + Prep Time: 1 1/2 hour

Ingredients:

- 4 half-cut chicken breasts, boneless, skinless
- Kosher salt ground pepper, as desired
- 1/2 cup of oil, olive

- 1 chopped onion, medium
- 1 tsp. of garlic, minced
- 1 tbsp. of minced, de-seeded chili, serrano
- 1/2 cup of cilantro, chopped
- 1 cup of corn
- 1 cup of green peas
- 1/2 chopped bell pepper, red
- 10 cups of broth, chicken
- 4 halved potatoes
- 1 cup of white rice, uncooked

Instructions:

1. Season chicken as desired. Heat oil in large pot on med-high. Add and stir serrano chili, onion and garlic. Cook till onion softens. Add chicken. Cook for five minutes more.

2. Add and stir red pepper, corn, peas and cilantro. Cook for a minute. Add chicken broth, rice and potatoes.

3. Bring to boil. Reduce the heat down to med-low. Simmer till potatoes are tender and chicken becomes opaque, about 40-45 minutes. Serve.

21 – Fried Plantain Chips

These chips are called chifles in Ecuador, and they're popular in Peru, too. They taste wonderful after they have been deep fried, then sprinkled with some salt.

Makes 4-6 Servings

Cooking + Prep Time: 25 minutes

Ingredients:

- 2 plantains, yellow-green
- To fry: 1 bottle oil, vegetable

- Salt, kosher, as desired

Instructions:

1. Slice off plantain ends. Peel the skin. Slice the plantains crossways in thin slices.

2. Heat 1-2 inches oil in sauce pan over med-high.

3. When oil has heated, fry in groups, a few plantain slices in each, one after another, till they are golden. Remove. Drain on plate with paper towels on it. Season as deserved and serve.

22 – Buttery Potatoes with Parsley

The fingerling potatoes in this recipe are tossed in butter and parsley. They make a delicious side dish that's also quick to prepare. They go great with meat or seafood.

Makes 4 Servings

Cooking + Prep Time: 1 hour 10 minutes

Ingredients:

- 5 potatoes, medium
- 1 tbsp. of oil, olive

- 1 tbsp. of butter, unsalted
- Salt, kosher
- Parsley, chopped

Instructions:

1. Wash the potatoes and peel them. Cut into similar sized cubes.

2. Cook potatoes in lots of salted, cold water. Once water is at a boil, cook for 10-15 minutes.

3. Remove and strain the potato cubes and allow them to cool.

4. Heat butter and oil in large sized pan on med-high. Place potatoes in one layer in pan. Allow them to sit without being disturbed for three to four minutes, till golden brown in color. Turn and repeat till all sides of cubes are a golden brown.

5. Turn heat off. Place potatoes in dish. Sprinkle with parsley and serve.

23 – Shrimp in Peanut Sauce

This stew is traditionally cooked over a stove first and then it's baked in a type of clay pot till a crust has formed on top. This is a quicker version, and the tastes still blend together wonderfully.

Makes 4 Servings

Cooking + Prep Time: 1/2 hour

Ingredients:

- 1 chopped onion, medium
- 1 diced pepper, green

- 2 chopped garlic cloves
- 1 tsp. of oregano, dried
- 1 pkg. of sazón Goya seasoning blend
- 1 small, chopped tomato
- 2 tbsp. of oil, vegetable
- 2 plantains, green
- 3 tbsp. of peanut butter, creamy
- 1 1/2 cups of chicken or fish stock
- 1 lb. of shrimp, peeled, medium
- 2 tbsp. of butter, unsalted
- 2 tbsp. of minced cilantro

Instructions:

1. Heat oil in large sized skillet on med. heat. Sauté onions, tomatoes, green peppers, oregano, garlic and the seasoning blend till mixture is fragrant and veggies are soft. This usually takes five to eight minutes. Remove veggies from the heat. Allow them to cool a bit.

2. Peel plantains. Place in food processor. Add stock slowly. Add sautéed vegetables. Process till fairly smooth and blended well.

3. Add shrimp to same skillet used above. Season as desired. Sauté in butter with cilantro till barely cooked. Set them aside.

4. Add vegetable mixture and plantain to skillet. Add and stir peanut butter. Then bring to simmer. Stir while cooking for 10 minutes or so, till mixture thickens.

5. Add the cooked shrimp to the sauce. Briefly stir till shrimp are heated fully through. Serve while warm on rice.

24 – Citrus Ceviche

This is one chef's take on a classic Ecuadorian ceviche. The citrus fruits are acidic, and this actually cooks the fish. It's especially refreshing on hot summer days.

Makes 4 Servings

Cooking + Prep Time: 2 3/4 hours

Ingredients:

- 1/2 cup of lemon juice, fresh
- 1/4 cup of lime juice, fresh
- 1/4 cup of orange juice, fresh
- 1 tsp. of fresh, grated ginger
- 2 tbsp. of oil, olive
- 1 lb. of 1/4"-thick sliced sea bass fillets
- 1/4 cup of chopped cilantro, fresh
- 1 sliced onion, medium
- 2 peeled, then pitted cubed avocados
- Kosher salt ground pepper, as desired
- 4 quartered, hard-boiled eggs, large

Instructions:

1. Combine oil, ginger, lime juice and lemon juice in medium sized glass or plastic bowl. Add bass. Toss and coat. Cover. Place in the fridge for two hours to marinate. Fish's flesh must be opaque and white.

2. Add avocado, cilantro and onion. Season as desired. Toss. Serve with hard-boiled eggs.

25 – Ecuadorian Cheesy Potato Soup

Locro de papa, or cheese and potato soup, is an Ecuadorian staple. It's usually topped with some avocado and served with spicy Aji sauce.

Makes 6 Servings

Cooking + Prep Time: 55 minutes

Ingredients:

- 1 chopped onion, large
- 2 minced garlic cloves
- 1 tbsp. of oil, vegetable
- 2 tbsp. of butter, unsalted

- 1 tsp. of cumin, ground
- 2 lbs. of potatoes, yellow
- 2 cups of chicken stock, low sodium
- 2 cups water, filtered
- 1/2 cup of cream
- 1/2 cup of milk, 2%
- 1 egg, large
- 5 oz. of grated cheese, Monterey Jack
- Optional, for garnishing: queso fresco cheese crumbles and diced avocado

Instructions:

1. Melt a tbsp. of butter a tbsp. of oil in heavy pot.

2. Add garlic and onion. Sauté the onions on low heat till they are soft, translucent and fragrant.

3. Peel potatoes. Cut in 1" cubes and set them aside.

4. When onions are golden and soft, add a cup of stock.

5. Remove the mixture to food processor. Process till it is a smooth, consistent puree and set it aside.

6. Add potatoes to heavy pot with other 1 tbsp. of butter. Sauté till potatoes are starting to turn a golden color.

7. Add the onion liquid back into pot with potatoes. Add another cup of stock, along with 2 cups of filtered water.

8. Bring the liquid to simmer. Season as desired. Cook the potatoes till they're tender, or 20-25 minutes. Mash potatoes well in pot.

9. Whisk egg with milk and cream in small sized bowl. Whisk cup of soup mixture in with cream and milk. Add all to soup pot and whisk to blend.

10. Whisk in cheese till it melts. Season soup as desired. Garnish with queso fresco cheese and avocado. Serve hot.

Ecuador boasts some magnificent desserts to tempt your taste beds. Here are a few...

26 – Dulce de Leche Alfajores

This dish is popular in all countries of Latin America, and there are many varieties. This type features crumbly, delicate butter cookies sandwiched with dulce de leche.

Makes 16 cookies

Cooking + Prep Time: 1 1/2 hour + 1 hour refrigeration time

Ingredients:

- 4 cups of flour, all purpose + extra for your work surface

- 1/4 cup + 2 tbsp. of sugar, powdered
- 1 1/2 cups of unsalted butter, chilled, cut in pieces
- 1/2 cup of water, filtered
- To sprinkle: sanding sugar
- Chilled Easy Dulce de Leche

Instructions:

1. Line cookie sheet with baking paper.

2. Sift powdered sugar and flour together. Pulse mixture with butter in food process till mixture looks like coarse meal.

3. Leave the food processor running and pour in the water slowly. Process till dough barely comes together.

4. Form dough into two flattened discs. Wrap them in cling wrap and place in refrigerator for an hour.

5. Preheat the oven to 350F. On floured work surface, roll out a disc of the dough to 1/4" thickness. Using 1 3/4" cookie cutter or cup, cut rounds out from dough. Transfer to cookie sheet. Repeat with the other dough disc. Gather up dough scraps reroll, then cut. Sprinkle 1/2 of rounds with the sanding sugar. Bake till golden. Transfer to wire rack and allow to completely cool.

6. 1/2 hour before you serve, spread 1-2 tsp. of dulce de leche on the bottom side of non-sugared cookies. Place the sugared cookies on the top and make sandwiches. Serve.

27 – Poached Figs

This is an easy, gluten-free, no-bake dessert that goes well after a filling meal. You can serve it with mascarpone or whipped cream.

Makes 4 Servings

Cooking + Prep Time: 1 1/4 hour

Ingredients:

- 2 cups of water, filtered
- 1/4 cup of honey, pure
- 2 tbsp. of sugar, granulated or brown

- 8 figs

Instructions:

1. Select a pan that is big enough to hold all your ingredients. Use it to heat the honey, sugar and water over med-high heat. Cook till sugar has dissolved. Lower heat down to med-low. Add the figs.

2. Allow the mixture to simmer till figs are tender. They should not be mushy. Turn them occasionally so all sides are poached.

3. Transfer figs to medium bowl with slotted spoon. Allow the honey and water to continue to simmer over med-low till liquid is reduced and the consistency thickens into a syrupy consistency. This takes about 12-15 additional minutes. Allow to cool.

4. Once figs have cooled a bit, remove their stems. Cut them in half. Serve.

28 – Ecuadorian Candied Squash

Also called Calabaza or dulce de zapallo, this dessert is made with pumpkin or squash simmered in a brown cane sugar syrup with spices. They are SO delicious, they disappear fast.

Makes 2-4 servings

Cooking + Prep Time: 1 hour 15 minutes

Ingredients:

- 1 small pumpkin or medium squash, 2 pounds or so
- 1 pound of panela (Mexican brown sugar), break into small chunks
- 5 sticks of cinnamon
- 5 small cloves
- 3 peppers, all spice
- 3 cups of water, filtered

Instructions:

1. Wash squash or pumpkin well. Then slice and open it. Remove membranes and seeds.

2. Slice squash into med. pieces. Place in large sized pot with panela chunks spices.

3. Add water. Bring to boil on med. heat. Boil for 1/2 hour with lid on.

4. Remove lid. Simmer for an hour or so, till the syrup has thickened.

5. Remove the mixture from heat. Serve warm.

29 – Ecuadorian Sweet Rolls

This buttery, sweet bread is served all over Latin America. It is typically shaped into rolls when prepared in Ecuador, then sprinkled with sugar.

Makes 30 Servings

Cooking + Prep Time: 3 3/4 hours

Ingredients:

- 6 1/2 cups of flour, bread
- 2 cups of milk, warm

- 1 1/2 tbsp. of dry yeast, active
- 2 eggs, large
- 8 tbsp. of butter, softened
- 1/2 cup of sugar, granulated
- 1 1/2 tsp. of salt, kosher

For topping

- 1 egg, large
- 2 tbsp. of butter, melted
- 1/4 cup of sugar, granulated

Instructions:

1. Place warm milk in bowl of standing mixer. Sprinkle in yeast. Set mixture to the side for five minutes, till yeast becomes bubbly.

2. Add sugar, 2 cups flour, 2 large eggs, butter and kosher salt. Use a dough hook on standing mixer to knead mixture till it is mixed well.

3. Gradually add the rest of the flour. Knead till you have a smooth, soft dough. You can use more or less flour, if needed.

4. Place dough in lightly oiled, large sized bowl. Allow it to rise at room temperature till it doubles in size. This usually takes about an hour and a half.

5. Preheat oven to 350F.

6. Divide dough into roughly 30 golf-ball sized pieces. Roll pieces into smooth balls. Place them with an inch between on large sized buttered cookie sheet.

7. Beat one egg lightly. Brush tops of rolls with the beaten egg.

8. Allow rolls to rise at room temperature till they are almost double their previous size. This takes about a half-hour.

9. Bake the rolls in 350F oven till golden brown color on the top, or 35-40 minutes or so. Brush tops with melted butter. Sprinkle with sugar and serve.

30 – Chocolate con Queso

This dish originated in Columbia, but has found a home in Ecuador, too. It pairs cheese and chocolate together. Sound weird? It tastes GREAT.

Makes 2 Servings

Cooking + Prep Time: 35 minutes

Ingredients:

- 34 fluid ounces of water or milk
- 6 tbsp. chocolate drink
- 1 ball mozzarella cheese

Instructions:

1. Pour milk into medium sized sauce pan.

2. Place pan on med. heat. Bring to a boil.

3. Add chocolate while constantly stirring.

4. Lower heat when mixture has begun bubbling.

5. Place cheese in cup. Pour hot chocolate on top of cheese.

6. Serve with corn cakes or bread.

Conclusion

This Ecuadorian cookbook has shown you…

How to use different ingredients to affect unique South American tastes in dishes both well-known and rare.

How can you include Ecuadorian specialties in your home recipes?

You can…

- Make sweet or savory breakfast dishes. They look like they would taste super, and you won't be disappointed.
- Learn to cook with pork, beef and chicken, which are used in various regions of Ecuador. They have many wonderful recipes prepared with meat.
- Enjoy making the delectable seafood dishes of Scandinavia, including bass and shrimp. Fish is popular in the coastal areas of Ecuador.
- Make dishes using plantains, which are often used in Ecuadorian cooking.

- Make various types of desserts like sweet rolls and poached figs that will tempt your family's sweet tooth.

Have fun experimenting! Enjoy the results!

Made in United States
Troutdale, OR
12/06/2024

25979758R00050